# The Pearson Lab Manual for Developing Writers

## Volume A: Sentences

## Linda Copeland

St. Louis Community College, Meramec

**Longman**

New York   Boston   San Francisco

London   Toronto   Sydney   Tokyo   Singapore   Madrid

Mexico City   Munich   Paris   Cape Town   Hong Kong   Montreal

The Pearson Lab Manual for Developing Writers: Volume A: Sentences

Copyright © 2010 Pearson Education, Inc.

4 5 6 7 8 9 10—BRR—11 10

Longman
is an imprint of

www.pearsonhighered.com

ISBN 10:     0 -205-63409-5

ISBN 13: 978-0-205-63409-5

# Preface

*The Pearson Lab Manual for Developing Writers* series has been designed as supplements for any developmental writing text organized along the rhetorical modes. The paragraph and essay workbook exercises illustrate key concepts and encourage students to apply these concepts, which are covered in most writing classes, i.e., audience, topic sentences, thesis statements, coherence, unity, and levels of development. The analysis exercises isolate concepts explained in class and in the primary text and allow students to demonstrate their understanding of these concepts. The building exercises allow students to apply the concepts and provide students with the "raw materials" to develop paragraphs and essays.

For many developmental students, the biggest hurdle to writing is simply coming up with something to say. Some of the paragraph and essay exercises provide much of the information, allowing the students to focus on articulating the main idea and developing organizing strategies. Other writing prompts encourage the students to develop their own ideas through guided prewriting exercises. The revision prompts direct the students' attention to specific key elements of their own writing and to assess whether they have met the needs of their reading audience. Throughout the paragraph and essay workbooks, audience and purpose stay at the forefront of the writing exercises.

The sentences workbook provides exercises that apply grammar, punctuation and mechanics rules rather than simply offer skills drills. Composing exercises that highlight specific sentence skills explained in the students' primary text make up most of the exercises. Even those exercises that require students to simply insert a punctuation mark or to choose between two words go further in requiring the student to provide the rationale behind the choices.

What all of the workbooks have in common is that they are built around topics that draw from history, science, popular culture and other areas that not only engage developmental students, but make them feel they are learning in a college-level academic community. The exercises are designed to be challenging, yet engaging and accessible.

# Sentences Workbook

## Table of Contents

# The Building Blocks of Sentences: Clauses and Phrases I

An **independent clause** has the three components necessary to make a complete sentence: a subject, a verb and a complete thought.  A **dependent clause** has a subject and a verb, but it does not express a complete thought.  A **phrase** is a group of words that has a subject or a verb, or it may have neither.

Identify each of the following groups of words as an independent clause (IC), a dependent clause (DC) or a phrase (P).

1. _____ although classes were cancelled
2. _____ running at top speed
3. _____ clean and fresh
4. _____ because Mikail loves a bargain
5. _____ the rain stopped
6. _____ if you decide to take the subway
7. _____ when the alarm sounded
8. _____ throwing off the covers and jumping out of bed
9. _____ a tall stern man
10. _____ the band played for two hours
11. _____ as the crowd dispersed
12. _____ chuckling softly to himself
13. _____ before Anne opened the door
14. _____ even though we were tired
15. _____ in the quiet of the summer night
16. _____ the soldier stood at attention
17. _____ since the dog kept barking all night long
18. _____ taking the long road back
19. _____ to hope for the best
20. _____ Hal trudged home after a long day

Choose any four of the phrases and dependent clauses and rewrite them as independent clauses.

1.



2.



3.



4.


*For more practice with clauses and phrases, go to www.mywritinglab.com...MyWritingLab...where better practice makes better writers!*

# The Building Blocks of Sentences: Clauses and Phrases II

An **independent clause** has the three components necessary to make a complete sentence: a subject, a verb and a complete thought. Tell why each of the following groups of words is not an independent clause.

1. followed the trail into the woods.
   a. missing a subject
   b. missing a verb
   c. missing a subject and a verb
   d. missing a complete thought
2. which is the reason I quit my job.
   a. missing a subject
   b. missing a verb
   c. missing a subject and a verb
   d. missing a complete thought
3. the child, peering through the keyhole
   a. missing a subject
   b. missing a verb
   c. missing a complete thought
   d. missing a verb and a complete thought
4. is hoping to do better on the next test
   a. missing a subject
   b. missing a verb
   c. missing a subject and a verb
   d. missing a verb and a complete thought
5. although the train was late
   a. missing a subject
   b. missing a verb
   c. missing a complete thought
   d. missing a verb and a complete thought
6. my boss, a very opinionated man
   a. missing a subject
   b. missing a verb
   c. missing a complete thought
   d. missing a verb and a complete thought
7. if the committee finishes the project on time
   a. missing a subject
   b. missing a verb
   c. missing a subject and a verb
   d. missing a complete thought
8. talked about her accomplishments
   a. missing a subject
   b. missing a verb
   c. missing a subject and a verb
   d. missing a complete thought
9. until the new software is installed
   a. missing a subject
   b. missing a verb
   c. missing a complete thought
   d. missing a verb and a complete thought
10. gripping the ball tightly, the home team pitcher
    a. missing a subject
    b. missing a verb
    c. missing a complete thought
    d. missing a verb and a complete thought

Once you have identified the missing part in each group, rewrite it as an independent clause.

1.

2.

3.

4.

5.

6.

7.

8.

9.

10.

2

# Compound Sentences I

Writers use compound sentences to connect two independent clauses that contain equally important ideas.

When the ideas are very closely related, and the writer wants to emphasize that connection, he or she might use only a semicolon to link the two clauses. Create compound sentences by linking the following independent clauses with only a semicolon.

1. Many students hear the information given in class. They do not always listen to it.

2. The mind processes information faster than the rate of normal speaking. A good listener must discipline the mind to stay focused.

3. Good listeners do not interrupt speakers. They listen carefully and avoid jumping to conclusions.

| **Coordinating Conjunctions** |
| --- |
| for |
| and |
| nor |
| but |
| or |
| yet |
| so |

**Adverbial Conjunctions**
accordingly
also
as a result
besides
consequently
for example
for instance
furthermore
however
in addition
indeed
in fact
instead
likewise
meanwhile
moreover
nevertheless
nonetheless
otherwise
then
therefore
thus

A writer may also connect the ideas in two independent clauses by using a comma and a coordinating conjunction. The conjunction should show how the ideas in the two clauses are related. Choose the best coordinating conjunction from the list on the left to join the following sets of independent clauses.

1. Good listening skills are essential in the classroom, _____ students should practice them whenever possible.

2. The front of the classroom is the most efficient place for good listening, _____ many students still sit in the back of the room.

3. Note-taking helps students organize what they hear, _____ organized information is easier to learn and remember.

Like coordinating conjunctions, adverbial conjunctions may also connect ideas in two independent clauses. However, these conjunctions require a semicolon before them and a comma after. Choose the best adverbial conjunction from the list on the left to join the following sets of independent clauses.

1. Some students mistakenly try to write down every word the instructor says; _____ , they have not really *listened* to the information.

2. Reading outside assignments before a lecture helps students prepare to be active listeners; _____, they are already able to anticipate important concepts and names likely to come up in the lecture.

3. Reading an assignment before a lecture also allows students to determine questions they may have about the material; _____, they can listen more closely to the lecture for answers to these questions.


Practice writing your own compound sentences about note-taking, listening to lectures, or other skills required of you as a student.

1. Write two compound sentences that join two independent clauses with only a semicolon.

   a.


   b.


2. Write two compound sentences that join two independent clauses with a coordinating conjunction and a comma.

   a.


   b.


3. Write two compound sentences that join two independent clauses with an adverbial conjunction. Don't forget to put a semicolon before the adverbial conjunction and a comma after it.

   a.


   b.


4

# Compound Sentences II

Write three compound sentences that support the following topic sentence:

My spring break was (or was not) very relaxing.

With each compound sentence, put a square around the conjunction and draw arrows pointing towards the additional punctuation you must use with the conjunction. Circle the subject and underline the verb in each independent clause.

Example:

(We) spent one day sampling the wines in Napa Valley, [and] the next day (we) explored the shops of Carmel.

1. Write a compound sentence by joining two simple sentences with a coordinating conjunction.

2. Write a compound sentence by joining two simple sentences with an adverbial conjunction.

3. Write a compound sentence by joining two simple sentences with a semicolon.

Write three compound sentences that support the following topic sentence:

Some people have acquired bad driving habits.

Again, with each compound sentence, put a square around the conjunction and draw arrows pointing towards the additional punctuation you must use with the conjunction. Circle the subject and underline the verb in each independent clause.

1. Write a compound sentence by joining two simple sentences with a coordinating conjunction.

2. Write a compound sentence by joining two simple sentences with an adverbial conjunction.

3. Write a compound sentence by joining two simple sentences with a semicolon.

*For more practice with compound sentences, go to www.mywritinglab.com...MyWritingLab...**where better practice makes better writers!***

# Complex Sentences I

A writer uses a complex sentence to show that one idea has more importance than another does. Express the less important idea in a dependent clause, and express the more important idea in an independent clause.

Example: When you look at the ideas expressed in the following two sentences, it is clear that one of the ideas is more important. A complex sentence would more clearly show this importance.

        Ernesto hiked the mountain trail.
    ✓ Ernesto did not see the rattlesnake.

As Ernesto hiked the mountain trail, **he did not see the rattlesnake**.
        **DC**                         **IC**

**Ernesto did not see the rattlesnake** as he hiked the mountain trail.
        **IC**                         **DC**

> Notice that if the dependent clause begins the sentence, you must follow it with a comma. If it is in the middle of the sentence, you do not need the comma

In the following exercise, first place a check by the sentence containing the idea you think is most important. Then combine the two ideas in a complex sentence that gives emphasis to the most important idea. Use the list of subordinating conjunctions to help you make one of the ideas a dependent clause.

| Subordinating Conjunctions |
| --- |
| after |
| although |
| as, as if |
| as long as |
| as though |
| because |
| before |
| even though |
| if, even if |
| in order that |
| rather than |
| since |
| so that |
| that |
| though |
| unless |
| until |
| when |
| whenever |
| where |
| wherever |
| whether |
| which |
| while |
| who |

1.  Thieves stole Vanessa's laptop computer and television.
    Vanessa forgot to lock her back door.

    _____

    _____

2.  Demonde trained for six months.
    Demonde ran his first marathon in under four hours.

    _____

    _____

3.  Keiko took her grandmother's old rug to the Antique Road Show.
    Keiko learned that the rug was worth $20,000.

    _____

    _____

4.  Kathy won $5 million in the state lottery.
    Kathy is my best friend's sister.

    _____

    _____

7

5. The rookie played in his first major league game.
   He hit the game-winning home run.

   _____

   _____

6. Addison checked her email on her laptop.
   The instructor reviewed the material to be covered on the exam.

   _____

   _____

7. The tornado devastated the town.
   There were no deaths or serious injuries.

   _____

   _____

8. Jared's beagle won Best in Show.
   Jared's raised and trained the dog himself.

   _____

   _____

9. My grandfather takes ginkgo biloba every day.
   My grandfather says ginkgo biloba helps his memory.

   _____

   _____

10. Construction workers were building a new downtown civic center.
    Construction workers uncovered the ruins of a 3,000-year-old prehistoric village.

   _____

   _____

8

# Complex Sentences II

Create complex sentences by adding independent clauses to the following dependent clauses.

1. After John reached his sales quota, _____
_____.

2. Because my car had a flat tire, _____
_____.

3. _____
_____, which is why I am celebrating.

4. Although Monica trained hard for the marathon,_____
_____.

5. _____
_____, where it is possible to be promoted.

6. When I tried to call the utility company to report a power outage,_____
_____.

7. _____
_____, who is the best candidate.

8. _____
_____as the crowd cheered.

9. If the heavy rains continue to fall, _____
_____.

10. Before the store opened, _____
_____.

11. _____
_____so that the building is wheelchair accessible.

12. _____
_____while Ethan filed the reports.

*For more practice with complex sentences, go to www.mywritinglab.com...MyWritingLab...**where better practice makes better writers!***

9

# Writing Compound and Complex Sentences

**Coordinating Conjunctions (FANBOYS)**
for
and
nor
but
or
yet
so

**Adverbial Conjunctions**
accordingly
also
as a result
besides
consequently
for example
for instance
furthermore
however
in addition
indeed
in fact
instead
likewise
meanwhile
moreover
nevertheless
nonetheless
otherwise
then
therefore
thus

**Subordinating Conjunctions**
after
although
as, as if
as long as
as though
because
before
even though
if, even if
in order that
rather than
since
so that
that
though
unless
until
when
whenever
where
wherever
whether
which
while
who

Your topic is cell phones.

1. Write a compound sentence that describes the convenience of cell phones. Use a coordinating conjunction to connect the two independent clauses.

_____

_____

_____

2. Write a compound sentence that describes some inappropriate behavior shown by some cell phone users. Use an adverbial conjunction to connect the two independent clauses.

_____

_____

_____

3. Write a complex sentence that describes how to go about choosing a cell phone provider. Begin the sentence with the dependent clause by using a subordinating conjunction.

_____

_____

_____

4. Write a complex sentence that states your position on using cell phones while driving. Begin the sentence with the independent clause.

_____

_____

_____

*For more practice with compound and complex sentences, go to www.mywritinglab.com...MyWritingLab...**where better practice makes better writers!***

10

# Fixing Comma Splices and Run-ons

| Coordinating Conjunctions |
|:---:|
| for |
| and |
| nor |
| but |
| or |
| yet |
| so |

**Comma Splice**: In the classroom a student can learn a lot about a particular field, an internship provides the opportunity to apply this knowledge in the workplace.

1. Connect the two independent clauses with a semicolon.

| Adverbial Conjunctions |
|:---:|
| accordingly |
| also |
| as a result |
| besides |
| consequently |
| for example |
| for instance |
| furthermore |
| however |
| in addition |
| indeed |
| in fact |
| instead |
| likewise |
| meanwhile |
| moreover |
| nevertheless |
| nonetheless |
| otherwise |
| then |
| therefore |
| thus |

2. Connect the independent clauses with a comma and coordinating conjunction.

3. Connect the independent clauses with a semicolon and adverbial conjunction followed by a comma.

4. Make one of the two independent clauses dependent (subordinate) by placing a subordinating conjunction in front of it. (DC, IC or IC DC)

**Run-on:** Employers often look for experience as well as education an internship can be a valuable addition to a resume.

1. Write the two independent clauses as two separate sentences.

| Subordinating Conjunctions |
|:---:|
| after |
| although |
| as, as if |
| as long as |
| as though |
| because |
| before |
| even though |
| if, even if |
| in order that |
| rather than |
| since |
| so that |
| that |
| though |
| unless |
| until |
| when |
| whenever |
| where |
| whereas |
| wherever |
| whether |
| which |
| while |
| who |

2. Connect the independent clauses with a comma and coordinating conjunction.

3. Connect the independent clauses with a semicolon and adverbial conjunction followed by a comma.

4. Make one of the two independent clauses dependent (subordinate) by placing a subordinating conjunction in front of it. (DC, IC or IC DC)

*For more practice with **Comma Splices and Run-ons**, go to www.mywritinglab.com... MyWritingLab... **where better practice makes better writers!***

**Commas I**

**I.** When two independent clauses are separated by a coordinating conjunction (for, and, nor, but, or, yet, so), a comma goes **before** the conjunction.

Example    Some people get tattoos as a way to express themselves artistically, and others may use tattoos to commemorate special events or people.

All of the following sentences contain coordinating conjunctions, but not all require commas. Put commas only in those sentences in which the coordinating conjunction separates two independent clauses.

1. The five thousand-year-old "ice man" discovered in the Alps had fifty-seven tattoos near acupuncture points on his body so scientists speculate these tattoos may have had a medicinal purpose.

2. Ancient Egyptians may have used tattoos to honor deities or to provide magical protection.

3. Samuel O'Reilly invented the tattoo machine in the late 1800s and the machines used today have changed very little since that time.

4. The tattoo machine punctures the skin as it injects ink so the artist must take precautions to prevent infection.

5. A tattoo appears to be on the outer layer of skin but the ink is actually injected into the second layer of skin.

6. Tattoo artists may create customized designs or they may use ready-made designs.

7. Seventeenth century Japanese used tattoos as punishment and identified criminals by tattooing their foreheads.

8. Reusable tattoo equipment is put in an autoclave after every use for that is the most effective means of sterilization.

9. Many people still associate tattoos with pirates and criminals yet a 2006 study by the American Academy of Dermatology found that nearly one in four Americans between the ages of eighteen and fifty are tattooed.

10.  The best tattoo parlors are clean and professional and the artist pays careful attention to safety precautions and health concerns.

**II.** Use a comma to set off transitional or introductory words, dependent clauses and long phrases that come at the beginning of sentences.

Examples:     For example, my brother had his girlfriend's name tattooed on his shoulder.
When his girlfriend broke up with him, my brother had a dragon tattooed over her name.
After seeing what happened to my brother, I decided to put off getting my own tattoo.

Add commas to the following sentences.

1. Before applying the needle the tattoo artist draws or traces a stencil of the design onto the client's skin.

2. Since the tattoo artists themselves are at risk for blood-transmitted diseases they must wear gloves during the procedure.

3. According to the Center for Disease Control there have been no documented cases of HIV being transmitted through tattooing.

4. However unsanitary tattooing practices have led to the transmission of Hepatitis B.

5.  In order to prevent the spread of disease tattoo artists follow the same bloodborne pathogens rules followed in hospitals and in doctors' offices.

6. Because some tattoo inks contain metallic pigments people have reported a burning pain during magnetic resonance imaging (MRI) exams.

7. When England's Prince of Wales received his first tattoo in 1862 he started a tattoo fad among the British aristocracy.

8.  Believing tattoos represent their spiritual power some Polynesian people add to and embellish their tattoos throughout their lives.

9.  Furthermore Polynesian tattoos are some of the world's most intricately detailed.

10. Ranked by *U.S. News & World Report* as one of the fastest growing industries of the '90s tattooing can be a lucrative profession for an artist.

**III.** Use commas to set off <u>nonrestrictive</u> words and phrases. <u>Nonrestrictive</u> means the word or phrase can be left out, and the meaning of the sentence will still be clear. Do not put commas around <u>restrictive</u> words and phrases. These are words and phrases that provide essential information about the subject.

Examples:

|  |  |
|---|---|
| (Nonrestrictive) | Tattooing, which began over five thousand years ago, is growing in popularity today. |
| (Restrictive) | Tattoos that show the slightest sign of infection should be checked by a doctor immediately. |

Add commas to the following sentences that contain nonrestrictive words and phrase. <u>Do not</u> put commas around restrictive phrases.

1. The Pazyryks who were iron age horsemen and warriors left spectacularly tattooed mummies.

2. After Maurice Berchon a French naval surgeon published a study in 1861 on the medical complications of tattoos, the French navy and army banned tattoos for servicemen.

3. The tattoo needle which punctures the skin between fifty and three thousand times per minute injects insoluble ink into the skin.

4. Tattoo artists who belong to professional organizations are more likely to know the latest trends and the most current safety precautions.

5. Tribal tattoos the most requested designs are based on the designs of Maori, Polynesian and Native American tribes.

6. Horace Ridler known as the Zebra Man had inch-wide zebra stripes tattooed allover his face and body.

7. People who are not up to date with their tetanus shots should not get tattoos.

8. A tattoo even after its fully healed is very sensitive to sunlight and should not be exposed to prolonged rays.

9. Some people who suffer from alopecia a hair loss condition may have eyebrows tattooed on.

10. It's important to remember that a new tattoo is essentially a wound which means it is susceptible to infection.

**IV.** Use commas to separate the parts of a series.

Examples:  A tattoo machine has four basic parts: a needle, a tube system, an electric motor and a foot pedal.

A large, fierce, green dragon tattoo covers my brother's upper arm.

1. Dragons stars wings and roses are popular tattoos for both men and women.

2. A mummy of a Pazyryk chieftain was covered with tattoos of deer goats griffins and fish.

3. Successfully removing a tattoo depends upon the age of the tattoo its size and the type of ink used in the tattoo.

4. The side effects of removing a tattoo can be infection scarring hypopigmentation or hyperpigmentation.

5. Some of the most painful areas for men to be tattooed are the abdomen the spine and the chest.

6.  People are tattooed most frequently on their backs necks arms wrists and ankles.

7. Maori tribesman created elaborate facial tattoos by dipping chisel-shaped pieces of bone shell or metal in pigment and then hitting them with a mallet.

8. The intricate delicate blue-black designs could completely cover a Maori warrior's face.

9. Those with medical conditions like heart disease diabetes skin disorders or immune deficiencies should not get tattoos.

10. Soldiers and sailors typically chose tattoo designs that represent courage patriotism and their loved ones.

## Commas II

Add any necessary commas to the following sentences. In the blank before the sentence write the letter of the comma rule that the sentence illustrates.

a. comma before a coordinating conjunction separating two independent clauses
b. comma setting off an introductory dependent clause, phrase or word
c. comma(s) setting off nonrestrictive word, phrase or dependent clause
d. comma(s) separating the parts of a series

____ 1. No one knows for certain when people first started chewing gum but we do know that chewing gum has been around for thousands of years.

____ 2. Ancient Greeks chewed mastiche a resin from the bark of the mastic tree.

____ 3. Like the Greeks the Mayans got their chewing gum from the sap of a tree.

____ 4. Chicle the sap of the sapodilla tree later became the main ingredient in the first modern chewing gum.

____ 5. The fresh soft flavorful gum we chew today is nothing like the first manufactured chewing gums.

____ 6. Before Thomas Adams began manufacturing chicle gum in 1870 Americans chewed sweetened paraffin wax.

____ 7. Adams tried to make a licorice-flavored chicle gum but the gum could not hold the flavor.

____ 8. By adding corn syrup and sugar to the chicle Adams was able to make a peppermint gum that held its flavor.

____ 9. Today's most popular gum flavors are cinnamon spearmint and peppermint.

____ 10. Walter Diemer who was an accountant for the Fleer Chewing Gum Company came up with the first successful recipe for bubblegum.

____ 11. Although the Fleer Company sold over a million dollars in bubble gum the first year Diemer received no royalties for his invention.

____ 12. People chew gum to relax to freshen their breath to resist the urge to snack or to smoke and to reduce discomfort when flying in an airplane.

____ 13. Over a thousand varieties of gum are manufactured and sold in the United States and Americans spend about a half billion dollars on gum every year.

____ 14. The record for the largest bubble ever blown which was set by Susan Montgomery Williams in 1994 is twenty-three inches in diameter.

____ 15. Because people were not properly disposing of gum the country of Singapore has banned the import and sale of chewing gum.

*For more practice with commas, go to www.mywritinglab.com... MyWritingLab...**where better practice makes better writers!***

16

# Composing with Commas

a.  comma before a coordinating conjunction separating two independent clauses
b.  comma setting off an introductory dependent clause, phrase or word
c.  comma(s) setting off  nonrestrictive word, phrase or dependent clause
d.  comma(s) separating the parts of a series

Compose each of the following sentences to illustrate the comma rule indicated.

1.  Write a sentence that names three activities you would enjoy doing while on vacation.
    (d)

2.  Write a sentence that describes two behaviors of a successful student. (a)

3.  Write a sentence that gives a nonrestrictive detail about a successful person you know.
    (c)

4.  Write a sentence that tells what you do to prepare for a test. (b)

5.  Write a sentence that tells how poor judgment can cause an accident. (b)

6.  Write a sentence that uses a series of adjectives to describe your favorite kind of
    sandwich. (d)

7.  Write a sentence that describes how two people perform the same task in different ways.
    (a)

8.  Write a sentence that includes the following dependent clause: which is why I am in
    college. (c)

17

# Subject-Verb Agreement

If a sentence has a singular subject, it must have a singular verb. If it has a plural subject, it must have a plural verb.

Example:    The <u>bird</u> <u>flies</u> across the sky.
            The <u>birds</u> <u>fly</u> across the sky.

            The <u>man</u> <u>works</u> long hours.
            The <u>men</u> <u>work</u> long hours.


How can you avoid subject-verb agreement errors?

**I.** First, be sure you know the difference between singular and plural verbs. (Helpful Tip: Most **s**ingular verbs end in <u>**s**</u>.) Circle the correct verb in each sentence, making sure it agrees in number with the subject. Draw an arrow from the verb you circle to the subject with which it agrees in number.


Example:    Student athletes (juggles, juggle) the demands of their sport and academics.


1. Those cars (runs, run) quite well on diesel fuel.

2. My car (is, are) a hybrid that gets excellent gas mileage.

3. On my campus, students (participates, participate) in service learning projects each semester.

4. Marcus (plans, plan) to work at a food pantry this summer.

5. The pin oak tree (sheds, shed) its leaves late in the fall.

6. Maple trees (lines, line) the streets of my town.

7. When stationed overseas, soldiers (appreciates, appreciate) receiving cards and letters from back home.

8. Every day Alaina (writes, write) to her brother, a Marine in Afghanistan.

9. The Hannah Montana concert (was, were) sold out the first day tickets went on sale.

10. Young girls (was, were) disappointed that they could not see Miley Cyrus live on stage.

18

**II.** Also, be sure you have correctly identified the subject of a sentence. Do not be confused by prepositional phrases that come between a subject and a verb. Circle the correct verb in each sentence, making sure it agrees in number with the subject. Cross out the prepositional phrase and draw an arrow from the verb you circle to the subject with which it agrees in number.

Example:    A box ~~of matches~~ (sits, sit) on the shelf by the fireplace.

1. A cloud of mosquitoes (rises, rise) from the dead leaves as I walk through the woods.
2. Delegates from across the state (votes, vote) for the candidates of their choice at the political convention.
3. The barking of the neighbor's dogs (keeps, keep) me awake at night.
4. Blocks of ice (forms, form) in the river when the temperatures drop below freezing.
5. A nest of baby robins (sits, sit) on the tree branch outside my window.
6. The movie star along with her entourage (plans, plan) to visit a local mall to promote her new perfume.
7. A bouquet of roses (is, are) left at Marilyn Monroe's grave every year on her birthday.
8. Tremors under the ocean floor (causes, cause) tidal waves called *tsunamis*.
9. The apartments on the third floor (is, are) always too hot in the summer.
10. Our galaxy with all its stars and planets (offers, offer) the hope of life beyond Earth.


**III.** Subjects joined by <u>and</u> are plural. Do not be confused by subjects joined by <u>or</u>, which are singular.

**George or Sam** <u>reads</u> the morning announcements. Only one boy reads.
(singular subject)

**George and Sam** <u>play</u> on the school's soccer team. Both boys play on the team.
(plural subject)

Circle the correct verb in each sentence, making sure it agrees in number with the subject.

1. The beagle or the Scottish terrier (is, are) sure to win Best in Show.
2. Mischa and Adam (is, are) spending spring break in Florida.
3. The English department and the math department (shares, share) classrooms in the same building.
4. Carrie or Alycia (has, have) the book you loaned to me.
5. Power lines and trees (falls, fall) down during heavy winds.
6. Reporters and photographers (tries, try) to get the latest scoop on popular celebrities.

19

7.  Mandy's mother or grandmother (drives, drive) her to preschool.

8.  Human error or a mechanical failure (causes, cause) most small plane crashes.

9.  My job and my homework (keeps, keep) me from spending more time with my friends.

10.  My neighbor's lawn mower or his barking dog (wakes, wake) me up each Sunday morning.

**IV.** Remember, a subject can come after the verb.  Even then, it must agree in number with the verb.  Circle the correct verb in each sentence, making sure it agrees in number with the subject.  Draw an arrow from the verb you circle to the subject with which it agrees in number.

Example:      Across the prairie (blows, blow) a howling wind.

1.  When I least expect it, up (jumps, jump) my cat onto my lap.

2.  Under my sofa cushion (was, were) popcorn kernels and two nickels.

3.  Just when I think I can concentrate on homework, here (comes, come) my friends, ready to play video games.

4.  Where (is, are) the tools I lent you to work on your car?

5.  Every spring, up (pops, pop) dandelions across my lawn.

6.  Recently, there (has, have) been reports of thefts in my neighborhood.

7.  Off in the distant sky (soars, soar) a lone eagle.

8.  On my desk (sits, sit) a picture of my grandmother.

9.  In the shadows by the hen house (lurks, lurk) a hungry fox.

10. By the side of the highway (sits, sit) a forlorn hitchhiker.

*For more practice with **subject-verb agreement**, go to www.mywritinglab.com... MyWritingLab...**where better practice makes better writers!***

# Pronoun-Antecedent Agreement

A pronoun must agree in number with its antecedent, the word the pronoun replaces.

>  Ava drove her mother to the doctor.

>  Mary and Bob took their essays to the writing center.

How can you avoid pronoun-antecedent agreement errors?

**I.** Don't be confused by subjects joined with or.

Examples:   Bill or Fred will read his essay aloud to the class.
Bill and Fred will read their essays aloud to the class.

1. Mike or Dave will borrow (his, their) parents' car to drive us to the lake.
2. Carrie or Sakina will bring (her, their) punch bowl for the party.
3. Drew and Carlos organized recycling in (his, their) neighborhood.
4. Antoinette and Maria joined (her, their) classmates in a service learning project.
5. Hannah or Olivia turned in a paper without (her, their) name on it.

**II.** Remember, the following indefinite pronouns are singular:

| (-one words) | (-body words) | (-thing words) | |
| --- | --- | --- | --- |
| one | nobody | anything | each |
| anyone | anybody | everything | every |
| everyone | everybody | nothing | either |
| someone | somebody | something | neither |

Examples:
(incorrect)   Every student is responsible for turning in their work on time.
(correct)   Every student is responsible for turning in his or her work on time.
**(better)   Students are responsible for turning in their work on time.

When you use indefinite pronouns, you must often resort to using wordy and awkward "he or she" or "him or her" constructions. To avoid these, use plurals in place of indefinite pronouns whenever possible.

1. Nobody in the company wants to lose (his or her, their) insurance benefits.
2. Either solution to the problem has (its, their) benefits and would be acceptable.
3. Someone left (his or her, their) umbrella in the theater.
4. Everybody in the Boy Scout troop did (his, their) part to clean up the park.
5. Each employee is expected to complete (his or her, their) online sexual harassment tutorial by June.
6. One of the actresses will take home an award for (her, their) performance.
7. Every kindergartener stood in line to have (his or her, their) vision tested.
8. Every parent at the PTO meeting said that school safety is (his or her, their) primary concern.

21

9. Since neither house passed (its, their) fire safety inspection, both were denied occupancy permits.
10. Everyone in the ballpark yelled at the top of (his or her, their) lungs when the home team scored the winning run.

Choose four of the above sentences that can be rewritten with plurals to make them less wordy and rewrite them.

Example:     1. The company's employees do not want to lose their insurance benefits.

_____     _____
          _____
          _____

_____     _____
          _____
          _____

_____     _____
          _____
          _____

_____     _____
          _____
          _____

*For more practice with **pronoun-antecedent agreement**, go to www.mywritinglab.com...
MyWritingLab...**where better practice makes better writers!***

# Pronoun Reference

**Part I.** A pronoun is a word that takes the place of a noun. The noun a pronoun replaces is called the pronoun's antecedent. In the following sentences, circle the pronouns and draw a line from the circled pronouns to their antecedents.

1. After Joaquin arrives home from school, he takes a short nap before going to work.

2. A French court found Mata Hari guilty of spying and executed her in 1917.

3. Japanese consider fugu a delicacy, but if not prepared properly, it can be deadly.

4. Best friends who room together in college sometimes encounter unexpected conflicts.

5. Tourists in Venice look forward to riding in gondolas, which have been used to transport people through the watery canals since the 11th century.

6. Actresses seldom kiss in Bollywood movies because they do not want to offend conservative fans.

7. Gary Gygax turned his love of games and the medieval period into the popular game *Dungeons and Dragons*.

8. When Queen Elizabeth I visited the Earl of Leicester, he honored her with a feast lasting seventeen days.

9. To avoid computer viruses, never open an email attachment unless you know the sender and were expecting it.

10. Although she is a single mother of two small children and holds a full-time job, Marjorie has maintained a 3.5 GPA in her college classes.

**Part II.** In each of the following sentences, there is a pronoun reference error because the pronoun does not clearly refer to a single antecedent. Rewrite the sentences to correct the errors.

1. Carlos and Joshua mailed in their FAFSA forms two months ago, but he hasn't heard back yet.

2. The Egyptians invented perfume because they believed their gods would be pleased if they smelled good.

3. In early melodramas, a male character would wear a cape and a mustache because it indicated he was a villain.

4. When Amelia and Sara entered their dogs in the show, hers won Best in Breed.

5. Brad worked as an intern over the summer and volunteered at a local food pantry, which will look good on his resume.

**Part III.** In each of the following sentences, there is a pronoun reference error because the antecedent is missing. Rewrite the sentences to correct the errors.

1. When running off the field at the end of an inning, they believe it is good luck to step on a base.

2. Mark is majoring in engineering because he always wanted to be one.

3. As I was driving down the highway, it said there was a rest stop ahead.

4. During the Middle Ages, Islamic monks cultivated coffee beans, but in Europe they would not drink it until Pope Clement VIII approved.

5. Because he had no close family members, President James Buchanan treated his cabinet like family and often invited them to dinner.

**Part IV.** Composing   Follow the directions to compose sentences with clear pronoun reference. In each sentence, circle the pronoun and draw an arrow to its antecedent.

1. Write a sentence that uses the pronoun *they* to refer to the people you've met at college.

2. Write a sentence that includes the names of two female celebrities and the pronoun *she* that clearly refers to one of the woman.

3. Write a sentence that contains the possessive pronoun *its* that clearly refers to an animal.

4. Write a sentence that contains the pronoun *which* that clearly refers to a vehicle you have driven.

5. Write a sentence that contains the names of two men and the pronoun *his* that clearly refers to one of the men.

6. Write a sentence that uses the pronoun *who* to refer to someone you have known for a long time.

*For more practice with **pronoun reference**, go to www.mywritinglab.com... MyWritingLab...**where better practice makes better writers!***

# Shifts in Person

Depending upon a writer's topic and purpose, three different "persons" can be used.

First person:        I  We
Second Person:    You (refers to the reader, **not** people in general)
Third Person:      Anyone who is not the writer or the reader–Bob, people, students, Eskimos, politicians, and so on.

Imagine that you are a successful salesperson.  Your boss has been so impressed with your work that she's asked you to write a brief description of what you do to make a sale.  You turn in the following **first person** account of how you make a sale:

## How I Make a Sale

When I set out to make a sale, I first get to know as much as possible about my prospective clients.  I do this by researching the company and by listening carefully to my clients.  In fact, I let them speak more than I do during a sales meeting, so I can learn as much about their company and its needs as possible.  I then start to build interest in my product by explaining how it will meet their needs and save their company money.  By keeping the focus on the benefits of our product, I let my clients know that I want their company to be more successful.  If my clients hesitate, I tell them how our product beats the competition and provide testimonials from our many satisfied customers.  While I am careful not to rush my clients, I urge them to act soon, so they can begin saving money.  Usually, helping my clients see the bottom line is all it takes to clinch the sale.

Your boss is so pleased that she asks you to write your technique up as a set of instructions for the other sales people.  Rewrite the paragraph as a set of instructions in **second person**.  The beginning has been started for you.

## How You Can Make a Sale

When **you** set out to make a sale, first **you** should get to know as much as possible about **your** prospective clients. _____

_____

_____

_____

_____

_____

_____

_____

_____

_____

_____

The response to your guidelines is so positive that your boss asks you to revise the paragraph yet again, so it can be published in the company newsletter. She wants the other employees to know what the company's salespeople do on the job and has asked that you rewrite the paragraph in **third person** so it refers to all the salespeople—men and women—at your company. The beginning has been started for you. (Watch pronoun reference as you revise this paragraph. *Salespeople* and *clients* are both plurals that the pronouns *they* and *their* might refer to.)

How They Make Their Sales

When our salespeople set out to make a sale, they first get to know as much as possible about the prospective clients. _____

_____
_____
_____
_____
_____
_____
_____
_____
_____
_____
_____

*For more practice with **shifts in person**, go to www.mywritinglab.com... MyWritingLab...**where better practice makes better writers!***

# Using Consistent Verb Tense
## Avoiding Unnecessary Shifts in Time

**Part I**. Circle the appropriate verb tense in each of the following sentences.

1. A media event that (captures, captured) the attention of the American public (is, was) the Sand Cave rescue of Kentucky spelunker Floyd Collins.

2. Today, the National Cave Rescue Commission (held, holds) eight-day training seminars in cave rescue, and a member of a cave rescue team (has, had) emergency medical training and experience in cave exploring.

3. In 1925, Floyd Collins (tries, tried) to find a new entrance to Mammoth Cave in order to attract tourists to his family's property.

4. Collins (finds, found) and (expands, expanded) an underground passage that he (thinks, thought) would open up into the underground caverns of Mammoth Cave.

5. On January 30, Collins (becomes, became) trapped in the passage when a rock (falls, fell) from the ceiling and (pins, pinned) his leg when he (is, was) only 150 feet from the entrance.

6. When a person (becomes, became) trapped in a cave, hypothermia (is, was) always a danger because most caves (have, had) a year-round temperature of about 54 degrees.

7. Because communication (is, was) difficult underground, rescuers today (use, used) special CB radios that (work, worked) through hundreds of feet of solid rock.

8. Friends (find, found) Collins the next day, and efforts (begin, began) to try to rescue him.

9. After the passage leading to Collins (collapse, collapsed) in two places, rescuers (start, started) to dig a new tunnel to reach him.

10. Falls (are, were) the primary cause of most cave injuries today followed by injuries (sustain, sustained) by rock falls.

**Part II.** Read the following sentences carefully and correct any faulty shifts in verb tense.

1. Newspaper reporter "Skeets" Miller from the *Louisville Courier-Journal* covered the rescue and wins a Pulitzer prize for the reports picked up by newspapers around the country.

2. Thousands of tourists came to the rescue site where vendors arrive to sell food and souvenirs.

3. People around the country hear regular reports of the rescue efforts on the radio, which was a relatively new media at that time.

27

4. Rescuers finally reached Collins on February 17 and find him dead from exposure and starvation.

5. His body was displayed in a glass-topped coffin in Crystal Cave until 1929 when vandals steal the body.

6. Collins' body is soon found, but the left leg was missing.

7. The body was then kept in a chained casket in Crystal Cave until the family buries it in Flint Cemetery in 1989.

**Part III.** The following paragraph describes a cave explorer's trip into a cavern as though it were happening right now in the present tense. Rewrite the passage in the past tense.

I carry my gear to the edge of the pit. I put on my harness and lower myself into the dark gloom of the cavern. For ten minutes I descend before I reach the bottom of the shaft. I walk upright through the first chamber of the cavern where stalagmites line the floor. As I walk farther into the chamber, the light from the top of the shaft fades, and the only light comes from the lantern mounted on my helmet. I pause to wait for my caving partners as they descend, and I take a long drink of water from my canteen. Even in this cool, wet cave I know I can become dehydrated quickly. Once my friends reach the bottom, we walk farther down the passage. We stop to look for a landmark to help us find our way back out. To our left, we see a rockfall, and in front of it a large stalagmite rising from the cave floor. We take the passage to the right of the rockfall. The passage shrinks to a crawl space. We crawl through the mud till the passage opens into a large chamber. Here we find pools of water. I shine my flashlight in the water and see fish. A pale salamander scampers from a rock into the water when it senses my presence. I turn my light to a cave formation on the wall that looks like a delicate drapery. Then I hear a shout from above. My friend Luke is on a ledge overlooking the pool chamber. "Rocks!" he shouts as his boots dislodge some stones from the ledge. My other caving partners and I cover our heads and quickly move away from the ledge. The rocks fall into the pool, and no one is hurt.

*For more practice with* **consistent verb tense**, *go to* www.mywritinglab.com... *MyWritingLab...***where better practice makes better writers!***

# Apostrophes

## Part I. Apostrophes in Contractions

Apostrophes indicate that one or more letters have been left out of a contraction. Add any necessary apostrophes to the contractions in the following sentences.

1. It isnt impossible to find the career thats best for you.

2. Dont try to decide too quickly or youre likely to decide upon the career you think you should want and not one that will make you truly happy.

3. Youll find clues to the right career by thinking about activities that make you happy or past accomplishments that made you most proud.

4. At this point, you shouldnt rule out careers because you think theyre not practical, or you lack necessary training.

5. Its important to discover your passions before assessing your skills, so you havent limited your possibilities.

Compose sentences that use the following words as contractions. The subject of your sentences should be the world of work. Write about jobs you've had or wish to have some day.

Example:     will not
             I **won't** settle for a job that I can't find fulfilling.

| | | | | |
|---|---|---|---|---|
| I am | I will | are not | who will | who is |
| has not | did not | could not | were not | of the clock |

## Part II. Apostrophes in Singular Possessives

An apostrophe and an s indicate ownership by a singular object or being. Do not be confused by plural words ending in s. These do not require apostrophes. Add any necessary apostrophes to the following sentences.

1. It is a good idea to look into some of the nations fastest-growing careers as you search for your ideal job.

2. The federal governments need for a variety of workers is strong even as other businesses downsize.

3. A persons interest in conserving resources could lead to an environmental career.

4. More medical professionals are needed as an aging populations demand for health care increases.

5.  A teachers job can be both fulfilling and secure, especially in high-demand fields like science and mathematics.

Compose sentences that use the singular possessive form of the following singular constructions.  Again, the subject of your sentences should be the world of work.

Example:      the work of a day
              After a **day's work**, I feel a sense of accomplishment.

the pay of a week          the salary of a woman        the expectations of a boss
the environment of an office  the cooperation of a spouse  the advantages of a degree
the security of a career    the success of an interview   the referral of a former
the attitude of a job-seeker                              employer

**Part III.  Apostrophes in Plural Possessives**  An apostrophe followed by an <u>s</u> indicates ownership by objects or beings (plural) if the word does not already end in <u>s</u>.  An apostrophe only indicates ownership by objects or beings (plural) if the word already ends in <u>s</u>.   Do not be confused by plural words ending in <u>s</u>.  These do not require apostrophes.  Add any necessary apostrophes to the following sentences.

1.  Paul was happy to learn his new job had excellent benefits and allowed three weeks vacation days the first year.

2.  Employees benefits can vary widely among jobs.

3.  When Maria decided to change careers, she sought experts advice.

4.  Womens opportunities to gain job skills through military service have increased significantly in past years.

5.  Drew followed several friends suggestions to look for jobs on various Internet sites.

Compose sentences that use the plural possessive form of the following plural nouns.  Again, the subject of your sentences should be the world of work.

Examples:     **hours**
              On a typical day, my boss expects two **hours'** overtime work from each employee.

              **children**
              My friend Kim found a job illustrating **children's** books.

employers    companies    men        teachers      parents
people       colleagues   customers  advisors      career center

*For more practice with* **apostrophes**, *go to* <u>www.mywritinglab.com</u>*... MyWritingLab...**where better practice makes better writers!***

30

# Dialogue

## Part I. Direct Quotes and Indirect Quotes

A direct quote tells exactly what someone said, using the person's exact words.  An indirect quote tells what was said, but does not use the person's exact words.  Only a direct quote has quotation marks in it.

Examples:    indirect--      Kendra said that her boss will not let her wear a nose ring at work.
               direct--        Kendra said, "My boss will not let me wear a nose ring at work."

Read the following sentences.  Add quotation marks to those that contain direct quotes.

1. Mr. Jenkins said that he would fire Kendra, but she is the best salesperson on his staff.

2. The district manager asked, Why would you want to fire someone who is so competent?

3. I just hate the way she dresses, and those tattoos on her arms are awful, replied Mr. Jenkins.

4. The district manager suggested that Mr. Jenkins was more concerned about Kendra's appearance than the customers, who seemed to like her.

5. Mr. Jenkins conceded that he might be able to reach a compromise.

6. I won't complain about Kendra's clothing if she keeps the tattoos covered and removes her nose ring during business hours, he said.

Now rewrite the three sentences that contain indirect quotes as direct quotes.

1.

2.

3.

Rewrite the three sentences that are direct quotes as indirect quotes.

1.

2.

3.

**Part II. Capitalizing and Punctuating Direct Quotes**  Look over the following examples of direct quotes.  Using these examples, answer the questions that follow, and you will come to understand the rules for capitalizing and punctuating direct quotes.

a.  "I really should fire Ed," **said the manager**.

b.  "What has Ed done to deserve being fired?" **asked the consultant**.

c.  **The manager replied**, "He's good at doing his work, but he can't get along with his co-workers.   He's very critical of others and often blames them for his mistakes."

d.  **After a pause, the consultant suggested**, "Have you considered offering a personal skills workshop?  All of your employees might benefit from some training."

e.  "That's a great idea!" **exclaimed the manager**.  "Can you arrange to set one up?"

f.  "I think," **said the consultant, looking at her schedule**, "that I can arrange for a workshop next week."

g.  **The manager said**, "Let's go ahead and schedule it."

First, notice the **tags**, which have been bolded in the sentences.  The **tag** is the part of a dialogue sentence that tells who is speaking and how the words are being said.

1.  A tag must be set off from the dialogue portion of the sentence.  What three punctuation marks can set off the tag?


2.  When must the first word in a tag be capitalized?



3.  Look at sentences **e** and **f**.  In sentence **e** the tag is followed by a period.  In sentence **f** it is followed by a comma.  Why?



Now look at the dialogue—the actual words spoken by the two people.  The dialogue is enclosed in quotation marks (" ").

1.  What do you notice about the first words in the spoken dialogue portion of the sentences?


2.  In sentence **f**, why is the word *that* not capitalized?


3.  What do you notice about the punctuation marks at the end of spoken dialogue in relation to the final quotation mark?

32

**Composing Practice** Use the following guidelines to compose a variety of different dialogue sentences. Your subjects for these sentences should be a continuation of one of the two workplace scenarios: Kendra's manner of dress and her boss's concern with it and/or the workshop to improve Ed's people skills. Be creative with your dialogue while following the rules for capitalization and punctuation.

1. Write a sentence that contains an indirect quote.

2. Write a sentence that contains a direct quote with the tag at the beginning of the sentence.

3. Write a sentence that contains a direct quote with the tag at the end of the sentence.

4. Write a sentence that uses a direct quote to ask a question.

5. Write a sentence that uses a direct quote that is an exclamation.

6. Write a sentence that has a tag in the middle of two direct quotes that are complete sentences.

7. Write a sentence that has a tag that interrupts a complete sentence.

*For more practice with **dialogue and quotation marks**, go to www.mywritinglab.com...*
*MyWritingLab...**where better practice makes better writers!***

# Capitalizing Proper Nouns

Each of the following writing tasks requires that you use proper nouns. Remember that proper nouns must be capitalized. Try to be creative with your sentences, adding descriptive details to make them interesting and informative.

Example:     Write a sentence that names your town or city and the name of a nearby river.

My home town of **St. Louis, Missouri** began as a **French** settlement along the banks of the **Mississippi River**.

1.  Write a sentence that gives the name of a person you know and the name of a sports team or civic organization of which that person is a member.

2.  Write a sentence that names a local high school or college and two foreign languages that are taught there.

3.  Write a sentence that names the nation of your birth and a holiday celebrated in that country.

4.  Write a sentence in which you tell the name of a magazine or book and the day of the week you could relax and read it. (Remember to put quotes around or underline the title of the literary work.)

5.  Write a sentence that names a television show and a name brand product that is typically advertised during commercials for that show. (Remember to underline the name of the television show.)

6.  Write a sentence that tells the month and day of your birth and the name of a local restaurant where you would like to have a celebratory birthday lunch.

7.  Write a sentence that names a specific company or business where you work or would like to work.

8.  Write a sentence that names an ocean you would like to see and the names of two people you would take with you to enjoy the beach.

9.  Write a sentence that gives the name of the current president and a senator. Be sure to use the titles with the names.

10. Write a sentence that gives the title (not just the type of course) of a specific memorable course you have taken in high school or college and the name of the instructor.

11. Write a sentence that gives the name of a busy street in your area and the names of two local businesses located on that street.

12. Write a sentence that includes the names of a least two world religions.

13. Write a sentence that names a war that the United States participated in that took place at least fifty years ago.

14. Write a sentence that includes the names of at least two national monuments found in the United States.

15. Write a sentence that names a grocery store and two name-brand products that could be found in your shopping cart.

*For more practice with **capitalization**, go to www.mywritinglab.com... MyWritingLab...**where better practice makes better writers!***

# Usage

**Part I.** Perhaps the most common usage errors involve confusing contractions with possessive pronouns. Remember, possessive pronouns do <u>not</u> contain apostrophes. Read the following sentences carefully and circle the correct pronoun or contraction.

1. A troglobite is an animal that spends (its, it's) entire life in a cave.
2. Jane Goodall observed chimpanzees using blades of grass to "fish" for (they're, their) food in termite mounds.
3. Creating a positive first impression increases (your, you're) chances of being hired.
4. A worker (whose, who's) environment is organized and pleasant will be more productive than a worker (whose, who's) in a stress-filled environment.
5. (Its, It's) possible to make a room more relaxing by painting it green.
6. Email attachments can spread viruses when (their, they're) opened.
7. (Your, You're) increasing (your, you're) chances of success by not taking too many classes during (your, you're) first semester.
8. According to Inuit hunters, (its, it's) more likely that a polar bear will be dangerous if more of (its, it's) ears are showing.
9. Writing students will find (their, they're) ability to succeed increases if (their, they're) willing to go to (their, they're) college's writing center for help with papers.
10. The author, (whose, who's) coming to campus next month, is the one (whose, who's) recent book made the best-seller list.

**Part II.** The following request for an extension on a written assignment might have been better received by the English teacher if the student had proofread it more carefully for usage errors. Read it carefully, correcting the twelve mistakes.

Dear Professor Allen,

My principle reason for righting you is to ask weather or not I can receive a short extension on my essay assignment. My dad thru his back out over the weekend, and I had to spend allot of time helping him get around the house. I know I should of notified you sooner, but it was to hectic around my house after my dad was injured, and their was no time I could call.

Before this assignment, I had a <u>A</u> average on my assignments. I would hate to loose the points on this assignment because of the negative affect that will have on my grade. I know you have given other students extra time on there papers, and I hope you will do the same for me.

Thank you,
Stuart

# ANSWER KEY

## The Building Blocks of Sentences: Clauses and Phrases I Key

An **independent clause** has the three components necessary to make a complete sentence: a subject, a verb and a complete thought.  A **dependent clause** has a subject and a verb, but it does not express a complete thought.  A **phrase** is a group of words that has a subject or a verb, or it may have neither.

Identify each of the following groups of words as an independent clause (IC), a dependent clause (DC) or a phrase (P).

1. __DC__    although classes were cancelled
2. __P__    running at top speed
3. __P__    clean and fresh
4. __DC__    because Mikail loves a bargain
5. __IC__    the rain stopped
6. __DC__    if you decide to take the subway
7. __DC__    when the alarm sounded
8. __P__    throwing off the covers and jumping out of bed
9. __P__    a tall stern man
10. __IC__    the band played for two hours
11. __DC__    as the crowd dispersed
12. __P__    chuckling softly to himself
13. __DC__    before Anne opened the door
14. __DC__    even though we were tired
15. __P__    in the quiet of the summer night
16. __IC__    the soldier stood at attention
17. __DC__    since the dog kept barking all night long
18. __P__    taking the long road back
19. __P__    to hope for the best
20. __IC__    Hal trudged home after a long day

Choose any four of the phrases and dependent clauses and rewrite them as independent clauses.

1.

2.

3.

4.

# The Building Blocks of Sentences: Clauses and Phrases II Key

An **independent clause** has the three components necessary to make a complete sentence: a subject, a verb and a complete thought. Tell why each of the following groups of words is not an independent clause.

1. followed the trail into the woods.
   **a. missing a subject**
   b. missing a verb
   c. missing a subject and a verb
   d. missing a complete thought
2. which is the reason I quit my job.
   a. missing a subject
   b. missing a verb
   c. missing a subject and a verb
   **d. missing a complete thought**
3. the child, peering through the keyhole
   a. missing a subject
   b. missing a verb
   c. missing a complete thought
   **d. missing a verb and/or a complete thought**
4. is hoping to do better on the next test
   **a. missing a subject**
   b. missing a verb
   c. missing a subject and a verb
   d. missing a verb and/or a complete thought
5. although the train was late
   a. missing a subject
   b. missing a verb
   **c. missing a complete thought**
   d. missing a verb and/or a complete thought
6. my boss, a very opinionated man
   a. missing a subject
   **b. missing a verb**
   c. missing a complete thought
   d. missing a verb and/or a complete thought
7. if the committee finishes the project on time
   a. missing a subject
   b. missing a verb
   c. missing a subject and a verb
   **d. missing a complete thought**
8. talked about her accomplishments
   **a. missing a subject**
   b. missing a verb
   c. missing a subject and a verb
   d. missing a complete thought
9. until the new software is installed
   a. missing a subject
   b. missing a verb
   **c. missing a complete thought**
   d. missing a verb and/or a complete thought
10. gripping the ball tightly, the home team pitcher
    a. missing a subject
    b. missing a verb
    c. missing a complete thought
    **d. missing a verb and/or a complete thought**

---

Once you have identified the missing part in each group, rewrite it as an independent clause.

1. Mark followed the trail into the woods.

2. I had to concentrate more on school, which is the reason I quit my job.

3. The child was peering through the keyhole.
or
The child, peering though the keyhole, saw Santa putting gifts under the tree.

4. Maria is hoping to do better on the next test.

5. Although the train was late, I still arrived in Chicago in time for the meeting.

6. My boss is a very opinionated man.

7. If the committee finishes the project on time, the company will do well this quarter.

8. Sara talked about her accomplishments.

9. Until the new software is installed, I can't run my computer.

10. Gripping the ball tightly, the home team pitcher went into his wind-up.

**Answers will vary.**

38

## Compound Sentences I Key

Writers use compound sentences to connect two independent clauses that contain equally important ideas.

When the ideas are very closely related, and the writer wants to emphasize that connection, he or she might use only a semicolon to link the two clauses. Create compound sentences by linking the following independent clauses with only a semicolon.

1. Many students hear the information given in class; they do not always listen to it.

2. The mind processes information faster than the rate of normal speaking; a good listener must discipline the mind to stay focused.

3. Good listeners do not interrupt speakers; they listen carefully and avoid jumping to conclusions.

| **Coordinating Conjunctions** | A writer may also connect the ideas in two independent clauses by using a comma and a coordinating conjunction. The conjunction should show how the ideas in the two clauses are related. Choose the best coordinating conjunction from the list on the left to join the following sets of independent clauses. |
|---|---|

**Coordinating Conjunctions**
for
and
nor
but
or
yet
so

A writer may also connect the ideas in two independent clauses by using a comma and a coordinating conjunction. The conjunction should show how the ideas in the two clauses are related. Choose the best coordinating conjunction from the list on the left to join the following sets of independent clauses.

1. Good listening skills are essential in the classroom, ___so___ students should practice them whenever possible.

2. The front of the classroom is the most efficient place for good listening, ___but___ many students still sit in the back of the room.

3. Note-taking helps students organize what they hear, ___and___ organized information is easier to learn and remember.

**Adverbial Conjunctions**
accordingly
also
as a result
besides
consequently
for example
for instance
furthermore
however
in addition
indeed
in fact
instead
likewise
meanwhile
moreover
nevertheless
nonetheless
otherwise
then
therefore
thus

Like coordinating conjunctions, adverbial conjunctions may also connect ideas in two independent clauses. However, these conjunctions require a semicolon before them and a comma after. Choose the best adverbial conjunction from the list on the left to join the following sets of independent clauses.

1. Some students mistakenly try to write down every word the instructor says; ___as a result___, they have not really *listened* to the information.

39

2. Reading outside assignments before a lecture helps students prepare to be active listeners;   consequently   , they are already able to anticipate important concepts and names likely to come up in the lecture.

3. Reading an assignment before a lecture also allows students to determine questions they may have about the material;        then        , they can listen more closely to the lecture for answers to these questions.

Practice writing your own compound sentences about note-taking, listening to lectures, or other skills required of you as a student. **Answers will vary.**

1. Write two compound sentences that join two independent clauses with only a semicolon.

    a.

    b.

2. Write two compound sentences that join two independent clauses with a coordinating conjunction and a comma.

    a.

    b.

3. Write two compound sentences that join two independent clauses with an adverbial conjunction. Don't forget to put a semicolon before the adverbial conjunction and a comma after it.

    a.

    b.

# Complex Sentences I Key

1.

    ✓ Thieves stole Vanessa's laptop computer and television.
    Vanessa forgot to lock her back door.

When Vanessa forgot to lock her back door, thieves stole her laptop computer and television.

2.

    Demonde trained for six months.
    ✓ Demonde ran his first marathon in under four hours.

Demonde, who trained for six months, ran his first marathon in under four hours.

3.

    Keiko took her grandmother's old rug to the Antique Road Show.
    ✓ Keiko learned that the rug was worth $20,000.

When Keiko took her grandmother's old rug to the Antique Road Show, she learned it was worth $20,000.

4.

    ✓ Kathy won $5 million in the state lottery.
    Kathy is my best friend's sister.

Kathy, who is my best friend's sister, won $5 million in the state lottery.

5.

    The rookie played in his first major league game.
    ✓ He hit the game-winning home run.

The rookie who was playing in his first major league game hit the game-winning home run.

6.

    Addison checked her email on her laptop.
    ✓ The instructor reviewed the material to be covered on the exam.

As Addison checked her email on her laptop, the instructor reviewed the material to be covered on the exam.

7.

    The tornado devastated the town.
    ✓ There were no deaths or serious injuries.

41

Although the tornado devastated the town, there were no deaths or serious injuries.

8.
   ✓ Jared's beagle won Best in Show.
   Jarod's raised and trained the dog himself.

Jarod's beagle, which Jarod raised and trained himself, won Best in Show.

9.
   My grandfather takes ginkgo biloba every day.
   ✓ My grandfather says ginkgo biloba helps his memory.

My grandfather says ginkgo biloba, which he takes every day, helps his memory.

10.
   Construction workers were building a new downtown civic center.
   ✓ Construction workers uncovered the ruins of a 3,000-year-old prehistoric village.

While they were building a new downtown civic center, construction workers uncovered the ruins of a 3,000-year-old prehistoric village.

# Complex Sentences II Key

**Answers will vary**.

1. After John reached his sales quota, **he celebrated by taking his best client out to lunch.**

2. Because my car had a flat tire, **I was late for class and missed a quiz**.

3. **This semester I earned enough credits to graduate,** which is why I am celebrating.

4. Although Monica trained hard for the marathon, **she sprained her ankle and could not complete the last two miles**.

5. **Andy moved to a different company**, where it is possible to be promoted.

6. When I tried to call the utility company to report a power outage, **the line was busy**.

7. **I am voting for Senator Jones**, who is the best candidate.

8. **The baseball player slid into home plate** as the crowd cheered.

9. If the heavy rains continue to fall, **the river is sure to flood.**.

10. Before the store opened, **customers lined up outside the doors**.

11. **Ramps and an elevator are being installed** so that the building is wheelchair accessible.

12. **Madison entered the data into the computer** while Ethan filed the reports.

# Fixing Comma Splices and Run-ons Key

<table>
<tr><td valign="top">

**Coordinating Conjunctions**
for
and
nor
but
or
yet
so

**Adverbial Conjunctions**
accordingly
also
as a result
besides
consequently
for example
for instance
furthermore
however
in addition
indeed
in fact
instead
likewise
meanwhile
moreover
nevertheless
nonetheless
otherwise
then
therefore
thus

**Subordinating Conjunctions**
after
although
as, as if
as long as
as though
because
before
even though
if, even if
in order that
rather than
since
so that
that
though
unless
until
when
whenever
where
whereas
wherever
whether
which
while
who

</td><td valign="top">

**Comma Splice**: In the classroom a student can learn a lot about a particular field, an internship provides the opportunity to apply this knowledge in the workplace.

1. Connect the two independent clauses with a semicolon.

In the classroom a student can learn a lot about a particular field; an internship provides the opportunity to apply this knowledge in the workplace.

2. Connect the independent clauses with a comma and coordinating conjunction.

In the classroom a student can learn a lot about a particular field, **but** an internship provides the opportunity to apply this knowledge in the workplace.

3. Connect the independent clauses with a semicolon and adverbial conjunction followed by a comma.

In the classroom a student can learn a lot about a particular field; **however,** an internship provides the opportunity to apply this knowledge in the workplace.

4. Make one of the two independent clauses dependent (subordinate) by placing a subordinating conjunction in front of it. (DC, IC or IC DC)

In the classroom a student can learn a lot about a particular field **whereas** an internship provides the opportunity to apply this knowledge in the workplace.

**Run-on:** Employers often look for experience as well as education an internship can be a valuable addition to a resume.

1. Write the two independent clauses as two separate sentences.

Employers often look for experience as well as education. **A**n internship can be a valuable addition to a resume.

2. Connect the independent clauses with a comma and coordinating conjunction.

Employers often look for experience as well as education, **so** an internship can be a valuable addition to a resume.

3. Connect the independent clauses with a semicolon and adverbial conjunction followed by a comma.

Employers often look for experience as well as education; **therefore,** an internship can be a valuable addition to a resume.

4. Make one of the two independent clauses dependent (subordinate) by placing a subordinating conjunction in front of it. (DC, IC or IC DC)

**Because** employers often look for experience as well as education, an internship can be a valuable addition to a resume.

</td></tr>
</table>

44

# Commas I Key

**I.** When two independent clauses are separated by a coordinating conjunction (for, and, nor, but, or, yet, so), a comma goes **before** the conjunction.

Example:     Some people get tattoos as a way to express themselves artistically, and others may use tattoos to commemorate special events or people.

All of the following sentences contain coordinating conjunctions, but not all require commas. Put commas only in those sentences in which the coordinating conjunction separates two independent clauses.

1. The five thousand-year-old "ice man" discovered in the Alps had fifty-seven tattoos near acupuncture points on his body, so scientists speculate these tattoos may have had a medicinal purpose.

2. Ancient Egyptians may have used tattoos to honor deities or to provide magical protection. **(no comma)**

3. Samuel O'Reilly invented the tattoo machine in the late 1800s, and the machines used today have changed very little since that time.

4. The tattoo machine punctures the skin as it injects ink, so the artist must take precautions to prevent infection.

5. A tattoo appears to be on the outer layer of skin, but the ink is actually injected into the second layer of skin.

6. Tattoo artists may create customized designs, or they may use ready-made designs.

7. Seventeenth century Japanese used tattoos as punishment and identified criminals by tattooing their foreheads. **(no comma)**

8. Reusable tattoo equipment is put in an autoclave after every use, for that is the most effective means of sterilization.

9. Many people still associate tattoos with pirates and criminals, yet a 2006 study by the American Academy of Dermatology found that nearly one in four Americans between the ages of eighteen and fifty are tattooed.

10.  The best tattoo parlors are clean and professional, and the artist pays careful attention to safety precautions and health concerns.

**II.** Use a comma to set off transitional or introductory words, dependent clauses and long phrases that come at the beginning of sentences.

Examples:   For example, my brother had his girlfriend's name tattooed on his shoulder.
When his girlfriend broke up with him, my brother had a dragon tattooed over her name.
After seeing what happened to my brother, I decided to put off getting my own tattoo.

Add commas to the following sentences.

1. Before applying the needle, the tattoo artist draws or traces a stencil of the design onto the client's skin.

2. Since the tattoo artists themselves are at risk for blood-transmitted diseases, they must wear gloves during the procedure.

3. According to the Center for Disease Control, there have been no documented cases of HIV being transmitted through tattooing.

4. However, unsanitary tattooing practices have led to the transmission of Hepatitis B.

5.  In order to prevent the spread of disease, tattoo artists follow the same bloodborne pathogens rules followed in hospitals and in doctors' offices.

6. Because some tattoo inks contain metallic pigments, people have reported a burning pain during magnetic resonance imaging (MRI) exams.

7. When England's Prince of Wales received his first tattoo in 1862, he started a tattoo fad among the British aristocracy.

8.  Believing tattoos represent their spiritual power, some Polynesian people add to and embellish their tattoos throughout their lives.

9.  Furthermore, Polynesian tattoos are some of the world's most intricately detailed.

10. Ranked by *U.S. News & World Report* as one of the fastest growing industries of the '90s, tattooing can be a lucrative profession for an artist.

**III.** Use commas to set off <u>nonrestrictive</u> words and phrases. <u>Nonrestrictive</u> means the word or phrase can be left out, and the meaning of the sentence will still be clear. Do not put commas around <u>restrictive</u> words and phrases. These are words and phrases that provide essential information about the subject.

Examples:

    (Nonrestrictive)        Tattooing, which began over five thousand years ago, is growing in popularity today.

    (Restrictive)            Tattoos that show the slightest sign of infection should be checked by a doctor immediately.

Add commas to the following sentences that contain nonrestrictive words and phrase. <u>Do not</u> put commas around restrictive phrases.

1. The Pazyryks, who were iron age horsemen and warriors, left spectacularly tattooed mummies.

2. After Maurice Berchon, a French naval surgeon, published a study in 1861 on the medical complications of tattoos, the French navy and army banned tattoos for servicemen.

3. The tattoo needle, which punctures the skin between fifty and three thousand times per minute, injects insoluble ink into the skin.

4. Tattoo artists who belong to professional organizations are more likely to know the latest trends and the most current safety precautions. **(restrictive)**

5. Tribal tattoos, the most requested designs, are based on the designs of Maori, Polynesian and Native American tribes.

6. Horace Ridler, known as the Zebra Man, had inch-wide zebra stripes tattooed allover his face and body.

7. People who are not up to date with their tetanus shots should not get tattoos. **(restrictive)**

8. A tattoo, even after it's fully healed, is very sensitive to sunlight and should not be exposed to prolonged rays.

9. Some people who suffer from alopecia, a hair loss condition, may have eyebrows tattooed on.

10. It's important to remember that a new tattoo is essentially a wound, which means it is susceptible to infection.

47

**IV.** Use commas to separate the parts of a series.

Examples: A tattoo machine has four basic parts: a needle, a tube system, an electric motor and a foot pedal.

A large, fierce, green dragon tattoo covers my brother's upper arm.

1. Dragons, stars, wings and roses are popular tattoos for both men and women.

2. A mummy of a Pazyryk chieftain was covered with tattoos of deer, goats, griffins and fish.

3. Successfully removing a tattoo depends upon the age of the tattoo, its size and the type of ink used.

4. The side effects of removing a tattoo can be infection, scarring, hypopigmentation or hyperpigmentation.

5. Some of the most painful areas for men to be tattooed are the abdomen, the spine and the chest.

6. People are tattooed most frequently on their backs, necks, arms, wrists and ankles.

7. Maori tribesman created elaborate facial tattoos by dipping chisel-shaped pieces of bone, shell or metal in pigment and then hitting them with a mallet.

8. The intricate, delicate blue-black designs could completely cover a Maori warrior's face.

9. Those with medical conditions like heart disease, diabetes, skin disorders or immune deficiencies should not get tattoos.

10. Soldiers and sailors typically chose tattoo designs that represent courage, patriotism and their loved ones.

# Commas II Key

Add any necessary commas to the following sentences. In the blank before the sentence write the letter of the comma rule that the sentence illustrates.

a. comma before a coordinating conjunction separating two independent clauses
b. comma setting off an introductory dependent clause, phrase or word
c. comma(s) setting off  nonrestrictive word, phrase or dependent clause
d. comma(s) separating the parts of a series

a     1. No one knows for certain when people first started chewing gum, but we do know that chewing gum has been around for thousands of years.

c     2. Ancient Greeks chewed mastiche, a resin from the bark of the mastic tree.

b     3. Like the Greeks, the Mayans got their chewing gum from the sap of a tree.

c     4. Chicle, the sap of the sapodilla tree, later became the main ingredient in the first modern chewing gum.

d     5. The fresh, soft, flavorful gum we chew today is nothing like the first manufactured chewing gums.

b     6. Before Thomas Adams began manufacturing chicle gum in 1870, Americans chewed sweetened paraffin wax.

a     7. Adams tried to make a licorice-flavored chicle gum, but the gum could not hold the flavor.

b     8. By adding corn syrup and sugar to the chicle, Adams was able to make a peppermint gum that held its flavor.

d     9. Today's most popular gum flavors are cinnamon, spearmint and peppermint.

c     10. Walter Diemer, who was an accountant for the Fleer Chewing Gum Company, came up with the first successful recipe for bubblegum.

b     11. Although the Fleer Company sold over a million dollars in bubble gum the first year, Diemer received no royalties for his invention.

d     12. People chew gum to relax, to freshen their breath, to resist the urge to snack or to smoke, and to reduce discomfort when flying in an airplane.

a     13. Over a thousand varieties of gum are manufactured and sold in the United States, and Americans spend about a half billion dollars on gum every year.

c     14.  The record for the largest bubble ever blown, which was set by Susan Montgomery Williams in 1994, is twenty-three inches in diameter.

b     15. Because people were not properly disposing of gum, the country of Singapore has banned the import and sale of chewing gum.

## Subject-Verb Agreement Key

**I.**

1. Those <u>cars</u> (runs, **run**) quite well on diesel fuel.

2. My <u>car</u> (**is**, are) a hybrid that gets excellent gas mileage.

3. On my campus, <u>students</u> (participates, **participate**) in service learning projects each semester.

4. <u>Marcus</u> (**plans**, plan) to work at a food pantry this summer.

5. The pin oak <u>tree</u> (**sheds**, shed) its leaves late in the fall.

6. Maple <u>trees</u> (lines, **line**) the streets of my town.

7. When stationed overseas, <u>soldiers</u> (appreciates, **appreciate**) receiving cards and letters from back home.

8. Every day <u>Alaina</u> (**writes**, write) to her brother, a Marine in Afghanistan.

9. The Hannah Montana <u>concert</u> (**was**, were) sold out the first day tickets went on sale.

10. Young <u>girls</u> (was, **were**) disappointed that they could not see Miley Cyrus live on stage.

**II.**

1. A <u>cloud</u> ~~of mosquitoes~~ (**rises**, rise) from the dead leaves as I walk through the woods.

2. <u>Delegates</u> ~~from across the state~~ (votes, **vote)** for the candidates of their choice at the political convention.

3. The <u>barking</u> ~~of the neighbor's dogs~~ (**keeps**, keep) me awake at night.

4. <u>Blocks</u> ~~of ice~~ (forms, **form**) in the river when the temperatures drop below freezing.

5. A <u>nest</u> ~~of baby robins~~ (**sits**, sit) on the tree branch outside my window.

6. The movie <u>star</u> ~~along with her entourage~~ (**plans,** plan) to visit a local mall to promote her new perfume.

7. A <u>bouquet</u> ~~of roses~~ (**is**, are) left at Marilyn Monroe's grave every year on her birthday.

8. <u>Tremors</u> ~~under the ocean floor~~ (causes, **cause**) tidal waves called *tsunamis*.

9. The <u>apartments</u> ~~on the third floor~~ (is, **are**) always too hot in the summer.

10. Our <u>galaxy</u> ~~with all its stars and planets~~ (**offers**, offer) the possibility of life beyond Earth.

**III.**

1. The beagle or the Scottish terrier (**is**, are) sure to win Best in Show.

2. Mischa and Adam (is, **are)** spending spring break in Florida.

3. The English department and the math department (shares, **share**) classrooms in the same building.

4. Carrie or Alycia (**has**, have) the book you loaned to me.

5. Power lines and trees (falls, **fall**) down during heavy winds.

6. Reporters and photographers (tries, **try**) to get the latest scoop on popular celebrities.

7. Mandy's mother or grandmother (**drives**, drive) her to preschool.

8. Human error or a mechanical failure (**causes**, cause) most small plane crashes.

9. My job and my homework (keeps, **keep**) me from spending more time with my friends.

10. My neighbor's lawn mower or his barking dog (**wakes**, wake) me up each Sunday morning.

**IV.**

1. When I least expect it, up (**jumps**, jump) my cat onto my lap.

2. Under my sofa cushion (was, **were**) popcorn kernels and two nickels.

3. Just when I think I can concentrate on homework, here (comes, **come**) my friends, ready to play video games.

4. Where (is, **are**) the tools I lent you to work on your car?

5. Every spring, up (pops, **pop**) dandelions across my lawn.

6. Recently, there (has, **have**) been reports of thefts in my neighborhood.

7. Off in the distant sky (**soars**, soar) a lone eagle.

8. On my desk (**sits**, sit) a picture of my grandmother.

9. In the shadows by the hen house (**lurks**, lurk) a hungry fox.

10. By the side of the highway (**sits**, sit) a forlorn hitchhiker.

# Pronoun-Antecedent Agreement Key

**I.** Don't be confused by subjects joined with <u>or</u>.

1. Mike or Dave will borrow (**his,** their) parents' car to drive us to the lake.
2. Carrie or Sakina will bring (**her**, their) punch bowl for the party.
3. Drew and Carlos organized recycling in (his, **their**) neighborhood.
4. Antoinette and Maria joined (her, **their**) classmates in a service learning project.
5. Hannah or Olivia turned in a paper without (**her,** their) name on it.

**II.** Remember, the following indefinite pronouns are singular:

1. Nobody in the company wants to lose (**his or her**, their) insurance benefits.
2. Either solution to the problem has (**its**, their) benefits and would be acceptable.
3. Someone left (**his or her**, their) umbrella in the theater.
4. Everybody in the Boy Scout troop did (**his**, their) part to clean up the park.
5. Each employee is expected to complete (**his or her**, their) online sexual harassment tutorial by June.
6. One of the actresses will take home an award for (**her**, their) performance.
7. Every kindergartener stood in line to have (**his or her**, their) vision tested.
8. Every parent at the PTO meeting said that school safety is (**his or her**, their) primary concern.
9. Since neither house passed (**its**, their) fire safety inspection, both were denied occupancy permits.
10. Everyone in the ballpark yelled at the top of (**his or her**, their) lungs when the home team scored the winning run.

4. All the Boy Scouts did their part to clean up the park.
5. Employees are expected to complete their online sexual harassment tutorials by June.
7. All the kindergarteners stood in line to have their vision tested.
8. All the parents at the PTO meeting said that school safety is their primary concern.
10. All the fans in the ballpark yelled at the top of their lungs when the home team scored the winning run.

# Pronoun Reference Key

**Part I.** A pronoun is a word that takes the place of a noun. The noun a pronoun replaces is called the pronoun's antecedent. In the following sentences, circle the pronouns and draw a line from the circled pronouns to their antecedents.

1. After Joaquin arrives home from school, he takes a short nap before going to work.

2. A French court found Mata Hari guilty of spying and executed her in 1917.

3. Japanese consider fugu a delicacy, but if not prepared properly it can be deadly.

4. Best friends who room together in college sometimes encounter unexpected conflicts.

5. Tourists in Venice look forward to riding in gondolas, which have been used to transport people through the watery canals since the 11th century.

6. Actresses seldom kiss in Bollywood movies because they do not want to offend conservative fans.

7. Gary Gygax turned his love of games and the medieval period into the popular game Dungeons and Dragons.

8. When Queen Elizabeth I visited the Earl of Leicester, he honored her with a feast lasting seventeen days.

9. To avoid computer viruses, never open an email attachment unless you know the sender and were expecting it.

10. Although she is a single mother of two small children and holds a full-time job, Marjorie has maintained a 3.5 GPA in her college classes.

**Part II.** In each of the following sentences, there is a pronoun reference error because the pronoun does not clearly refer to a single antecedent. Rewrite the sentences to correct the errors.

1. Carlos and Joshua mailed in their FAFSA forms two months ago, but **Carlos** [OR **Joshua**] hasn't heard back yet.

2. The Egyptians invented perfume because they believed their gods would be pleased if **the Egyptians** smelled good.

3. In early melodramas, a male character would wear a cape and a mustache because **they** indicated he was a villain.

53

4. When Amelia and Sara entered their dogs in the show, **Amelia's** [OR **Sara's**] won Best in Breed.

5. Brad worked as an intern over the summer and volunteered at a local food pantry, **which will both** look good on his resume.

**Part III.** In each of the following sentences, there is a pronoun reference error because the antecedent is missing. Rewrite the sentences to correct the errors.

1. When running off the field at the end of an inning, **baseball players** believe it is good luck to step on a base.

2. Mark is majoring in engineering because he always wanted to be **an engineer**.

3. As I was driving down the highway, **a sign** said there was a rest stop ahead.

4. During the Middle Ages, Islamic monks cultivated coffee beans, but in Europe **people** would not drink **coffee** until Pope Clement VIII approved.

5. Because he had no close family members, President James Buchanan treated his cabinet like family and often invited **the members** to dinner.

**Part IV.** Composing   Follow the directions to compose sentences with clear pronoun reference. In each sentence, circle the pronoun and draw an arrow to its antecedent.

1. Write a sentence that uses the pronoun *they* to refer to the people you've met at college.

2. Write a sentence that includes the names of two female celebrities and the pronoun *she* that clearly refers to one of the woman.

3. Write a sentence that contains the possessive pronoun *its* that clearly refers to an animal.

4. Write a sentence that contains the pronoun *which* that clearly refers to a vehicle you have driven.

5. Write a sentence that contains the names of two men and the pronoun *his* that clearly refers to one of the men.

6. Write a sentence that uses the pronoun *who* to refer to someone you have known for a long time.

**Answers will vary.**

54

# Shifts in Person Key

Depending upon a writer's topic and purpose, three different "persons" can be used.

    First person:          I  We

    Second Person:      You (refers to the reader, **not** people in general)

    Third Person:       Anyone who is not the writer or the reader–Bob, people, students, Eskimos, politicians, and so on.

Imagine that you are a successful salesperson. Your boss has been so impressed with your work that she's asked you to write a brief description of what you do to make a sale. You turn in the following **first person** account of how you make a sale:

## How I Make a Sale

When I set out to make a sale, I first get to know as much as possible about my prospective clients. I do this by researching the company and by listening carefully to my clients. In fact, I let them speak more than I do during a sales meeting, so I can learn as much about their company and its needs as possible. I then start to build interest in my product by explaining how it will meet their needs and save their company money. By keeping the focus on the benefits of our product, I let my clients know that I want their company to be more successful. If my clients hesitate, I tell them how our product beats the competition and provide testimonials from our many satisfied customers. While I am careful not to rush my clients, I urge them to act soon, so they can begin saving money. Usually, helping my clients see the bottom line is all it takes to clinch the sale.

Your boss is so pleased that she asks you to write your technique up as a set of instructions for the other sales people. Rewrite the paragraph as a set of instructions in **second person**. The beginning has been started for you.

## How You Can Make a Sale

When **you** set out to make a sale, first **you** should get to know as much as possible about **your** prospective clients. You should research the company and listen carefully to **your** clients. In fact, let them speak more than **you** do during a sales meeting, so **you** can learn as much about their company and its needs as possible. **You** can then start to build interest in the product by explaining how it will meet their needs and save their company money. By keeping the focus on the benefits of the product, **you** can let **your** clients know that **you** want their company to be more successful. If the clients hesitate, **you** should tell them how the product beats the competition and provide testimonials from **your** many satisfied customers. While being careful not to rush the clients, **you** should urge them to act soon, so they can begin saving money. Usually, helping the clients see the bottom line is all it takes to clinch the sale.

The response to your guidelines is so positive that your boss asks you to revise the paragraph yet again, so it can be published in the company newsletter. She wants the other employees to know what the company's salespeople do on the job and has asked that you rewrite the paragraph in **third person** so it refers to all the salespeople—men and women—at your company. The beginning has been started for you. (Watch pronoun reference as you revise this paragraph. *Salespeople* and *clients* are both plurals that the pronouns *they* and *their* might refer to.)

How Our Salespeople Make Their Sales

When our salespeople set out to make a sale, they first get to know as much as possible about the prospective clients. **They** do this by researching the clients' company and by listening carefully to **the** clients. In fact, clients speak the most during a sales meeting, so **the salespeople** can learn as much about the **clients'** company and its needs as possible. **Our salespeople** then start to build interest in our product by explaining how it will meet the **clients'** needs and save their company money. By keeping the focus on the benefits of our product, **our salespeople** let the clients know that **we** want their company to be more successful. If the clients hesitate, **the salespeople** tell them how our product beats the competition and provide testimonials from our many satisfied customers. While **our salespeople** are careful not to rush, the clients are urged to act soon, so they can begin saving money. Usually, helping the clients see the bottom line is all it takes to clinch the sale.

**NOTE: Answers may vary.**

## Using Consistent Verb Tense
## Avoiding Unnecessary Shifts in Time Key

**Part I**. Circle the appropriate verb tense in each of the following sentences.

1. A media event that **captured** the attention of the American public **was** the Sand Cave rescue of Kentucky spelunker Floyd Collins.

2. Today, the National Cave Rescue Commission **holds** eight-day training seminars in cave rescue, and a member of a cave rescue team **has** emergency medical training and experience in cave exploring.

3. In 1925, Floyd Collins **tried** to find a new entrance to Mammoth Cave in order to attract tourists to his family's property.

4. Collins **found** and **expanded** an underground passage that he **thought** would open up into the underground caverns of Mammoth Cave.

5. On January 30, Collins **became** trapped in the passage when a rock **fell** from the ceiling and **pinned** his leg when he **was** only 150 feet from the entrance.

6. When a person **becomes** trapped in a cave, hypothermia **is** always a danger because most caves **have** a year-round temperature of about 54 degrees.

7. Because communication **is** difficult underground, rescuers today **use** special CB radios that **work** through hundreds of feet of solid rock.

8. Friends **found** Collins the next day, and efforts **began** to try to rescue him.

9. After the passage leading to Collins **collapsed** in two places, rescuers **started** to dig a new tunnel to reach him.

10. Falls **are** the primary cause of most cave injuries today followed by injuries **sustained** by rock falls.

**Part II.** Read the following sentences carefully and correct any faulty shifts in verb tense.

1. Newspaper reporter "Skeets" Miller from the *Louisville Courier-Journal* covered the rescue and **won** a Pulitzer prize for the reports picked up by newspapers around the country.

2. Thousands of tourists came to the rescue site where vendors **arrived** to sell food and souvenirs.

3. People around the country **heard** regular reports of the rescue efforts on the radio, which was a relatively new media at that time.

4. Rescuers finally reached Collins on February 17 and **found** him dead from exposure and starvation.

5. His body was displayed in a glass-topped coffin in Crystal Cave until 1929 when vandals **stole** the body.

6. Collins' body **was** soon found, but the left leg was missing.

7. The body was then kept in a chained casket in Crystal Cave until the family **buried** it in Flint Cemetery in 1989.


**Part III.** The following paragraph describes a cave explorer's trip into a cavern as though it were happening right now in the present tense. Rewrite the passage in the past tense.

I **carried** my gear to the edge of the pit. I put on my harness and **lowered** myself into the dark gloom of the cavern. For ten minutes I **descended** before I reach the bottom of the shaft. I **walked** upright through the first chamber of the cavern where stalagmites **lined** the floor. As I **walked** farther into the chamber, the light from the top of the shaft **faded**, and the only light **came** from the lantern mounted on my helmet. I **paused** to wait for my caving partners as they **descended**, and I **took** a long drink of water from my canteen. Even in this cool, wet cave I **knew** I **could** become dehydrated quickly. Once my friends **reached** the bottom, we **walked** farther down the passage. We **stopped** to look for a landmark to help us find our way back out. To our left, we **saw** a rockfall, and in front of it a large stalagmite rising from the cave floor. We **took** the passage to the right of the rockfall. The passage **shrank** to a crawl space. We **crawled** through the mud till the passage **opened** into a large chamber. Here we **found** pools of water. I **shined** my flashlight in the water and **saw** fish. A pale salamander **scampered** from a rock into the water when it **sensed** my presence. I **turned** my light to a cave formation on the wall that **looked** like a delicate drapery. Then I **heard** a shout from above. My friend Luke **was** on a ledge overlooking the pool chamber. "Rocks!" he **shouted** as his boots **dislodged** some stones from the ledge. My other caving partners and I **covered** our heads and quickly **moved** away from the ledge. The rocks **fell** into the pool, and no one **was** hurt.

# Apostrophes Key

## Part I. Apostrophes in Contractions

Apostrophes indicate that one or more letters have been left out of a contraction. Add any necessary apostrophes to the contractions in the following sentences.

1. It **isn't** impossible to find the career **that's** best for you.

2. **Don't** try to decide too quickly or **you're** likely to decide upon the career you think you should want and not one that will make you truly happy.

3. **You'll** find clues to the right career by thinking about activities that make you happy or past accomplishments that made you most proud.

4. At this point, you **shouldn't** rule out careers because you think **they're** not practical, or you lack necessary training.

5. **It's** important to discover your passions before assessing your skills, so you **haven't** limited your possibilities.

Compose sentences that use the following words as contractions. The subject of your sentences should be the world of work. Write about jobs you've had or wish to have some day.

Example:      will not
          I **won't** settle for a job that I can't find fulfilling.

| I am | I will | are not | who will | who is |
|------|--------|---------|----------|--------|
| has not | did not | could not | were not | of the clock |

## Part II. Apostrophes in Singular Possessives

An apostrophe and an <u>s</u> indicate ownership by a singular object or being. Do not be confused by plural words ending in <u>s</u>. These do not require apostrophes. Add any necessary apostrophes to the following sentences.

1. It is a good idea to look into some of the **nation's** fastest-growing careers as you search for your ideal job.

2. The federal **government's** need for a variety of workers is strong even as other businesses downsize.

3. A **person's** interest in conserving resources could lead to an environmental career.

4. More medical professionals are needed as an aging **population's** demand for health care increases.

5. A **teacher's** job can be both fulfilling and secure, especially in high-demand fields like science and mathematics.

59

Compose sentences that use the singular possessive form of the following singular constructions. Again, the subject of your sentences should be the world of work.

Example:    the work of a day
            After a **day's work**, I feel a sense of accomplishment.

week's pay              woman's salary                boss's expectation
office's environment    spouse's cooperation          degree's advantage
career's security       interview's success           former employer's referral
job-seeker's attitude

**Part III. Apostrophes in Plural Possessives** An apostrophe followed by an <u>s</u> indicates ownership by objects or beings (plural) if the word does not already end in <u>s</u>. An apostrophe only indicates ownership by objects or beings (plural) if the word already ends in <u>s</u>. Do not be confused by plural words ending in <u>s</u>. These do not require apostrophes. Add any necessary apostrophes to the following sentences.

1. Paul was happy to learn his new job had excellent benefits and allowed three **weeks'** vacation days the first year.

2. **Employees'** benefits can vary widely among jobs.

3. When Maria decided to change careers, she sought **experts'** advice.

4. **Women's** opportunities to gain job skills through military service have increased significantly in past years.

5. Drew followed several **friends'** suggestions to look for jobs on various Internet sites.

Compose sentences that use the plural possessive form of the following plural nouns. Again, the subject of your sentences should be the world of work.

Examples:    **hours**
             On a typical day, my boss expects two **hours'** overtime work from each
employee.

             **children**
             My friend Kim found a job illustrating **children's** books.

employers'    companies'    men's        teachers'    parents'
people's      colleagues'   customers'   advisors'    career centers'

# Dialogue Key

**Part I. Direct Quotes and Indirect Quotes**

A direct quote tells exactly what someone said, using the person's exact words. An indirect quote tells what was said, but does not use the person's exact words. Only a direct quote has quotation marks in it.

Examples:    indirect--    Kendra said that her boss will not let her wear a nose ring at work.
             direct--      Kendra said, "My boss will not let me wear a nose ring at work."

Read the following sentences. Add quotation marks to those that contain direct quotes.

1. Mr. Jenkins said that he would fire Kendra, but she is the best salesperson on his staff.

2. The district manager asked, "Why would you want to fire someone who is so competent?"

3. "I just hate the way she dresses, and those tattoos on her arms are awful," replied Mr. Jenkins.

4. The district manager suggested that Mr. Jenkins was more concerned about Kendra's appearance than the customers, who seemed to like her.

5. Mr. Jenkins conceded that he might be able to reach a compromise.

6. "I won't complain about Kendra's clothing if she keeps the tattoos covered and removes her nose ring during business hours," he said.

Now rewrite the three sentences that contain indirect quotes as direct quotes.

1. Mr. Jenkins said, "I would fire Kendra, but she is the best salesperson on my staff."

2. "You may be more concerned about Kendra's appearance than your customers, who seem to like her," the district manager suggested.

3. "Maybe I can compromise," Mr. Jenkins conceded.

Rewrite the three sentences that are direct quotes as indirect quotes.

1. The district manager asked why Mr. Jenkins would fire someone who is so competent.

2. Mr. Jenkins replied that he hated the way Kendra dresses and her tattoos.

3. Mr. Jenkins said that he wouldn't complain about Kendra's clothing as long as she keeps her tattoos covered and removes her nose ring during business hours.

61

**Part II. Capitalizing and Punctuating Direct Quotes**  Look over the following examples of direct quotes.  Using these examples, answer the questions that follow, and you will come to understand the rules for capitalizing and punctuating direct quotes.

a.  "I really should fire Ed," **said the manager**.

b.  "What has Ed done to deserve being fired?" **asked the consultant**.

c.  **The manager replied**, "He's good at doing his work, but he can't get along with his co-workers.   He's very critical of others and often blames them for his mistakes."

d.  **After a pause, the consultant suggested**, "Have you considered offering a personal skills workshop?  All of your employees might benefit from some training."

e.  "That's a great idea!" **exclaimed the manager**.  "Can you arrange to set one up?"

f.  "I think," **said the consultant, looking at her schedule**, "that I can arrange for a workshop next week."

g.  **The manager said**, "Let's go ahead and schedule it."

First, notice the **tags**, which have been bolded in the sentences.  The **tag** is the part of a dialogue sentence that tells who is speaking and how the words are being said.

1.  A tag must be set off from the dialogue portion of the sentence.  What three punctuation marks can set off the tag?

Comma, question mark and exclamation point

2.  When must the first word in a tag be capitalized?

When a tag begins a sentence, it should be capitalized.

3.  Look at sentences **e** and **f**.  In sentence **e** the tag is followed by a period.  In sentence **f** it is followed by a period.  Why?

In sentence **e** the tag ends a complete sentence.  In sentence **f** the tag interrupts a complete sentence.

Now look at the dialogue—the actual words spoken by the two people.  The dialogue is enclosed in quotation marks (" ").

1.  What do you notice about the first words in the spoken dialogue portion of the sentences?

The first word of spoken dialogue should always be capitalized.

2.  In sentence **f**, why is the word *that* not capitalized?

It is a continuation of the sentence begun with "I think."

62

3. What do you notice about the punctuation marks at the end of spoken dialogue in relation to the final quotation mark?

The quotation mark encloses the punctuation.

**Composing Practice** Use the following guidelines to compose a variety of different dialogue sentences. Your subjects for these sentences should be a continuation of one of the two workplace scenarios: Kendra's manner of dress and her boss's concern with it and/or the workshop to improve Ed's people skills. Be creative with your dialogue while following the rules for capitalization and punctuation.

1. Write a sentence that contains an indirect quote.

2. Write a sentence that contains a direct quote with the tag at the beginning of the sentence.

3. Write a sentence that contains a direct quote with the tag at the end of the sentence.

4. Write a sentence that uses a direct quote to ask a question.

5. Write a sentence that uses a direct quote that is an exclamation.

6. Write a sentence that has a tag in the middle of two direct quotes that are complete sentences.

7. Write a sentence that has a tag that interrupts a complete sentence.

**Answers will vary.**

# Usage Key

**Part I.** Perhaps the most common usage errors involve confusing contractions with possessive pronouns. Remember, possessive pronouns do <u>not</u> contain apostrophes. Read the following sentences carefully and circle the correct pronoun or contraction.

1. A troglobite is an animal that spends **its** entire life in a cave.
2. Jane Goodall observed chimpanzees using blades of grass to "fish" for **their** food in termite mounds.
3. Creating a positive first impression increases **your** chances of being hired.
4. A worker **whose** environment is organized and pleasant will be more productive than a worker **who's** in a stress-filled environment.
5. **It's** possible to make a room more relaxing by painting it green.
6. Email attachments can spread viruses when **they're** opened.
7. **You're** increasing **your** chances of success by not taking too many classes during **your** first semester.
8. According to Inuit hunters, **it's** more likely that a polar bear will be dangerous if more of **its** ears are showing.
9. Writing students will find **their** ability to succeed increases if **they're** willing to go to **their** college's writing center for help with papers.
10. The author, **who's** coming to campus next month, is the one whose recent book made the best-seller list.


**Part II.** The following request for an extension on a written assignment might have been better received by the English teacher if the student had proofread it more carefully for usage errors. Read it carefully, correcting the twelve mistakes.

Dear Professor Allen,

My **principal** reason for **writing** you is to ask **whether** or not I can receive a short extension on my essay assignment. My dad **threw** his back out over the weekend, and I had to spend **a lot** of time helping him get around the house. I know I **should have** notified you sooner, but it was **too** hectic around my house after my dad was injured, and **there** was no time I could call.

Before this assignment, I had **an** <u>A</u> average on my assignments. I would hate to **lose** the points on this assignment because of the negative **effect** that will have on my grade. I know you have given other students extra time on **their** papers, and I hope you will do the same for me.

Thank you,
Stuart

**Sentence Skills Workbook Resources**

Compound Sentences—Listening Skills
http://www.coping.org/dialogue/listen.htm
http://www.connectionsmagazine.com/articles/4/061.html
http://www.kishwaukeecollege.edu/learning_skills_center/study_skills_help/good_listener.shtml
Commas—Tattoos
http://www.thehistoryof.net/the-history-of-body-piercings.html
www.vanishingtattoo.com
http://kidshealth.org/teen/your_body/skin_stuff/safe_tattooing.html
Commas II—chewing gum
http://inventors.about.com/od/gstartinventions/a/gum.htm
http://www.ideafinder.com/history/inventions/bubblegum.htm
http://recipes.howstuffworks.com/question86.htm/printable
http://www.nacgm.org/consumer/funfacts.html


Pronoun Reference—Miscellaneous
Perfume-- http://www.thehistoryof.net/the-history-of-perfume.html
Gondolas-- http://www.fodors.com/world/europe/italy/venice/feature_30005.html
Queen Elizabeth-- http://www.trivia-library.com/famous-fabulous-feasts-in-history/index.htm
Bollywood-- http://www.bollywoodworld.com/whatisbollywood/
Sports Superstition—http://www.factmonster.com/spot/superstitions1.html
Coffee--
http://www.associatedcontent.com/article/574455/clement_viii_the_pope_who_popularized.html
James Buchannon-- http://www.picturehistory.com/find/c/352/mcms.html
Shifts in Person—making a sale
http://communication.howstuffworks.com/sales-technique3.htm
Consistent Verb Tense—Cave Exploring
www.**exploringcaves**.com
 http://www.cave-exploring.com/Hazards.htm
http://www.onrock.co.uk/ExploringCaves.html
http://www.advancedrt.com/articles/rtarticles/cave.html
http://www.geocities.com/Athens/Olympus/4631/archcave.htm
http://en.wikipedia.org/wiki/Floyd_Collins_(person)
http://www.roadsideamerica.com/story/2105


Apostrophes—Finding a job
http://www.helpguide.org/life/finding_career.htm
http://www.quintcareers.com/printable/finding_career_passion.html
http://www.cbsnews.com/stories/2008/06/02/business/marketwatch/printable4147710.shtml#